Catholicism
FOR EVERYBODY

written by
Monica Ashour

designed by
David Fiegenschue & **Emily Gudde**

Level 8
BOOK 2
Second Edition

Dedicated to the Church, including our family and friends, and especially to Mother Mary and Saint John Paul. Tremendous thanks to all TOBET members over the years. Special thanks to Aly, Amy, Christopher, Colleen, Emily, Joseph, Kathy, Patrick, Sheryl, Véronique, and Zoe. We are grateful for consultation work by the translator of the *Theology of the Body*, Dr. Michael Waldstein, as well as Dr. Susan Waldstein. We are also grateful for the consultation work of Katrina J. Zeno, MTS.

For my parents, nieces & nephews, and St. John of the Cross

Nihil Obstat: Tomas Fuerte, S.T.L.
Censor Librorum

Imprimatur: +Most Reverend Samuel J. Aquila, S.T.L.
Archbishop of Denver
Denver, Colorado, USA
Feast of the Chair of St. Peter the Apostle • February 22, 2020

Library of Congress information on file. ISBN 978-1-945845-39-0 • Second Edition
Cover Design: FigDesign • Layout: Emily Gudde • Editor: Dayspring Brock • Associate Editor: Alexis Mausolf

Excerpts from the English translation of the *Catechism of the Catholic Church*. New York: Catholic Book Publishing Co., 1994.
Based on John Paul II's *Man and Woman He Created Them: A Theology of the Body*. Trans. Michael Waldstein, Copyright © 2006. Used by permission of Pauline Books & Media, 50 Saint Paul's Ave, Boston, Massachusetts 02130. All rights reserved. www.pauline.org.
All Scripture verses are from the *New American Bible*, Revised Edition (NABRE)
Some ideas in Lesson 1 based on Hahn, Scott. *Kinship by Covenant: A Canonical Approach to the Fulfillment of God's Saving Promises*. New Haven, CT: Yale University Press, 2009. Used with permission.
The quote on p. 11 on the right is from Pope Benedict XVI. *Benedictus*. Ed. Rev. Peter John Cameron, O.P. (San Francisco: Magnificat/ Ignatius Press, 2006), www.ignatius.com. Used with permission.
The quote on p. 38 is from Ratzinger, Joseph Cardinal. *The Spirit of the Liturgy* (p.181). San Francisco: Ignatius Press, 2000. Used with permission.
The quote on p. 41 is from Pope Benedict XVI. "Meditation on the Veneration of the Holy Shroud." Pastoral Visit to Turin, May 2, 2010. Rome: The Holy See, http://www.vatican.va/content/benedict-xvi/en/speeches/2010/may/documents/hf_ben-xvi_spe_20100502_meditazione-torino.html.
Image Credits: Shutterstock: pg 42 ©ThamKC / pg 46 ©suns07butterfly • Getty Images: pg 48 ©Keystone/Hulton Archive

Printed in the United States of America. © Copyright 2021 Monica Ashour. All rights reserved. No part of this book may be reproduced or transmitted in any form or by any means, electronic or mechanical, including photocopying, recording, or by any information storage and retrieval system without permission in writing from the publisher.

Table of Contents

1 ## Covenants of Life and Love 4
- The original covenant of life and love is found in the Holy Trinity.
- God extends covenants to humanity throughout salvation history.
- Two significant covenants are marriage and the union of Christ and His Church.

2 ## Sacraments EmBODY Covenant 14
- Catholics have a sacramental view of reality.
- God's people encounter Him bodily through the sacraments.
- A proper understanding of marriage leads to a better understanding of all the sacraments.

3 ## The Body as Prophet 26
- EveryBODY is meant to be a prophet of God's love.
- False prophets take neither the body nor science seriously.
- The Catholic Church is a prophet to the world.

4 ## The Center of Catholicism 38
- The cross is the sign of the New and Eternal Covenant.
- Christ's suffering on the cross leads to the joy of Easter.
- The center of Catholicism is the body—the Body of Christ.

1 Covenants of Life and Love

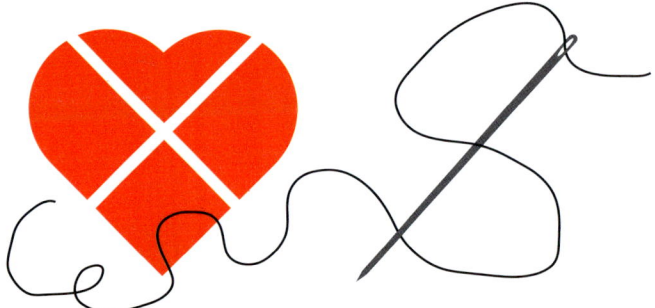

The Truth of Covenants

"Cross my heart, hope to die, stick a needle in my eye!" Have you ever heard someone make this promise? It comes from an ancient pledge which specifies that if the pledge is ever broken, the one that broke it would allow his heart to be cut into four quarters and his eyes to be poked out! Of course, you should not take this pledge literally, but nevertheless, it makes an important point. Promises should always be kept. Even more sacred than a promise, though, is a covenant.

Promises last until they are fulfilled, but covenants stand forever. A covenant is mutual giving, an exchange. It is not just an exchange of ideas, goods, or even affection. A covenant is an exchange of persons; each person in a covenant says, "I give myself to you." This exchange is enduring and profound. Did you know that you entered into your first covenant at Baptism? That marks your adoption into God's family. God reaches His people through covenant.

God IS Covenant

God's eternal, hidden mystery is the union and communion of the three Persons of the Trinity. God the Father, God the Son, and God the Holy Spirit are each Gifts to and for each other, forming **the** original covenant of life and love.

AnyBODY who gives the gift of self participates in God's covenant of life and love. Covenant is key. There are two covenants in particular that remind us that we are made for love: **1)** the covenant of marriage; and, **2)** the covenant of Christ and His Church. These are enduring and profound bonds, for they are based on truth and love.

This book is an overview of what it means to be Catholic. For those of you who have read other books from *The Body Matters*, you are familiar with concepts like the gift of self, reverence, friendship, and purity of heart. Now you are ready to synthesize the Catholic Faith from a Theology of the Body perspective.

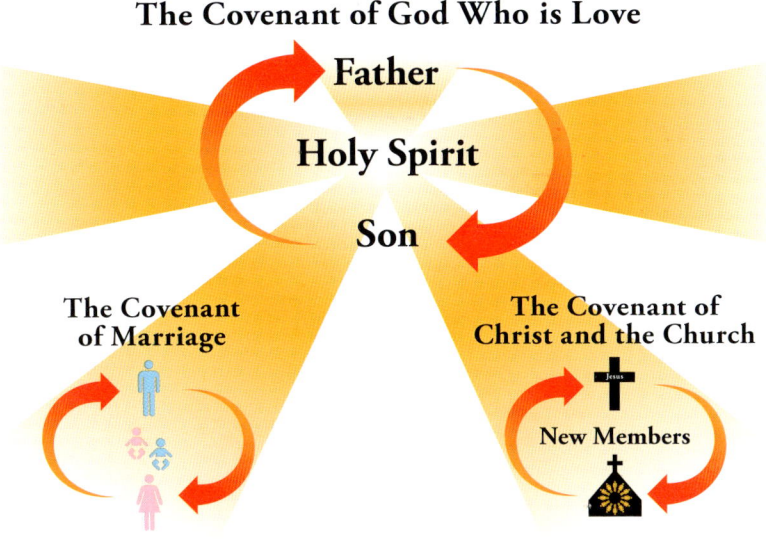

© Copyright 2021 by Monica Ashour. All rights reserved.

"God is love, and whoever remains in love remains in God and God in him."
1 Jn. 4:16

The Covenant of Marriage

God wants to make sure that everyBODY knows that all people are invited to be in covenant with Him, not just those who hear the Gospel proclaimed. That's why He gave us an obvious sign of covenant—marriage.

Did you know that marriage and family life have existed in all cultures throughout history? God gave us the gift of marriage as a sign of union and communion. As a couple lives out their covenant of marriage, they reflect God's hidden mystery of life and love to the world. When a husband and wife mutually give to and receive from each other, their union brings God's covenant to bear on Earth, and they might be blessed with a child, a sign of new life.

By understanding the meaning of marriage, we can understand more about our Catholic Faith and more about God Himself.

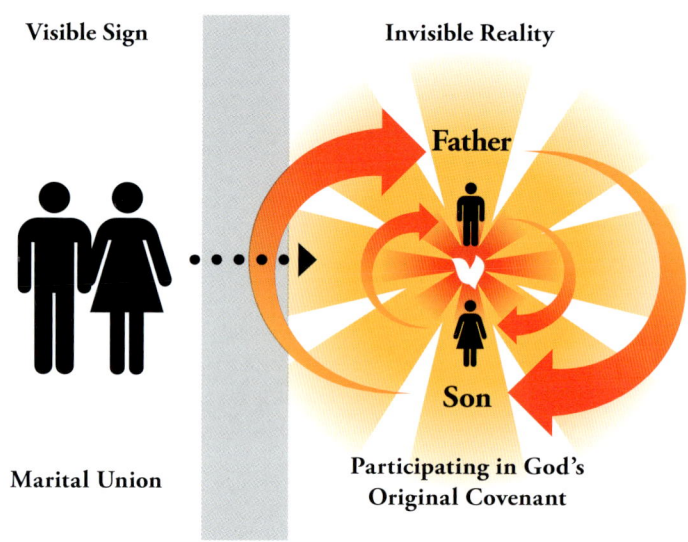

"[Marriage is] *understood as a sign that* efficaciously *transmits in the visible world the invisible mystery hidden in God from eternity.*"
Theology of the Body 19:4

God's Covenant with Humans

God has revealed the theme of covenant throughout salvation history. God made the first covenant with Adam and all of creation on the seventh day. (The word *seven* in Hebrew means "sacred bond.") He promised to remain faithful to all of creation, especially to His people. Then He gave Adam and Eve to each other to live in covenantal marriage. And you know how that story goes, don't you?

God was faithful to His covenant with Adam and Eve, but they broke their covenant with Him and with each other, bringing disunion to all subsequent generations. Yet God did not give up. Although they did not honor their covenant, God honored His, even extending the covenant to their descendants—Noah, Abraham, Moses, and David.

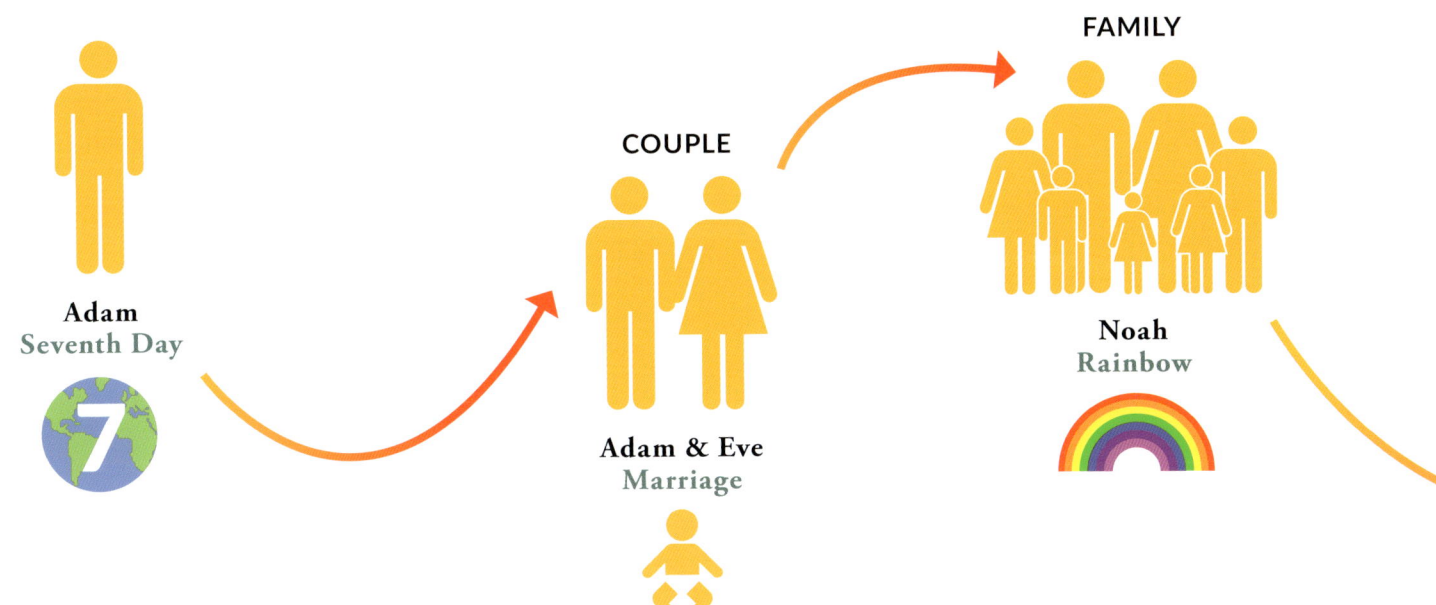

Visible Signs of Invisible Covenants

For each of His covenants in history, God provides a **visible** sign to represent His **invisible** faithfulness. For instance, God put a **visible** rainbow in the sky as a sign of His **invisible** covenant with Noah to never again flood the Earth. In another example, God gave Moses the **visible** Ten Commandments as a sign of His **invisible** moral law of love.

God made many covenants with His people. Yet, just like Adam and Eve, none of those who entered into covenant with God remained faithful to Him. Eventually, each generation also sinned and broke the covenant. What—or who—could stop this line of broken covenants?

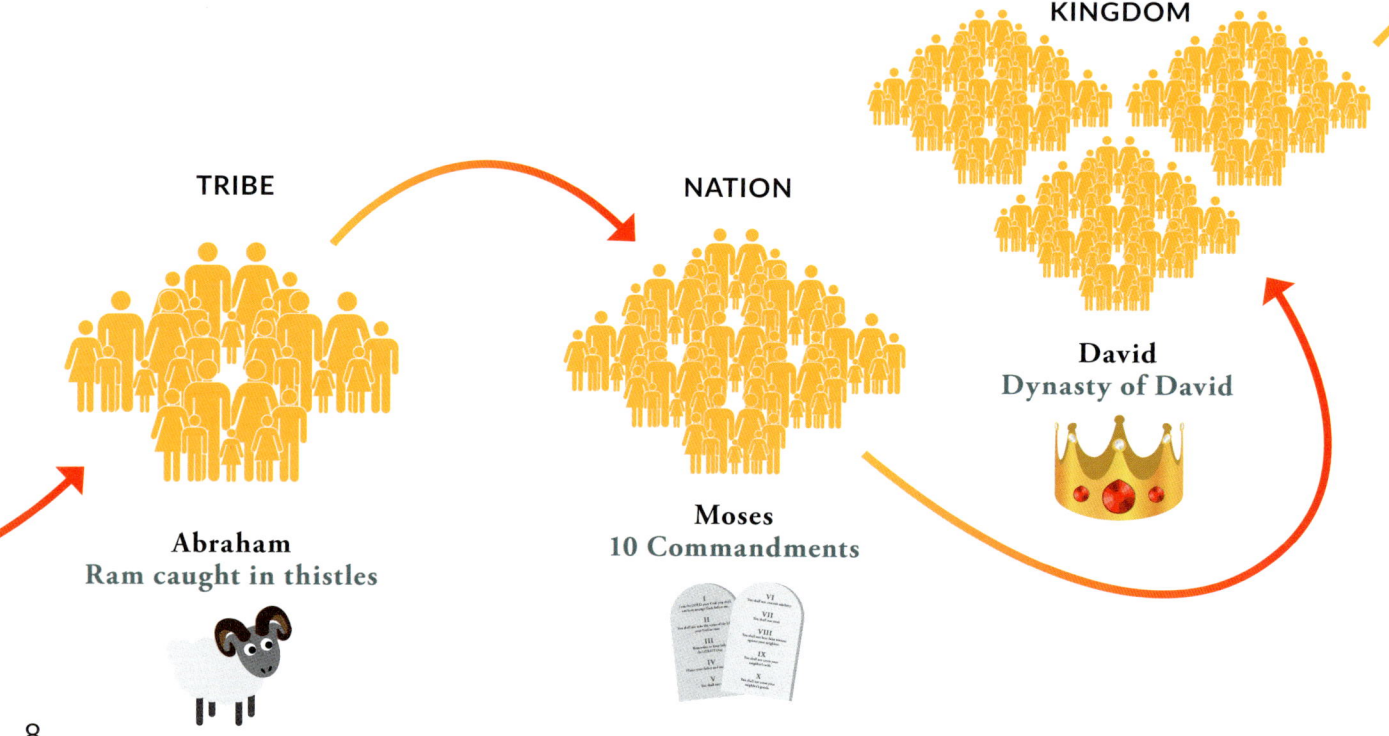

The Covenant of Christ and His Church

It was God Himself Who would at last break the pattern of human unfaithfulness. How? Divinity touched humanity when God the Son entered the world and became one with us. Jesus restored our covenant with God by His Gift of Self on the cross.

Christ's sacrifice restores our union and communion with God the Father through the **visible** Church. Jesus gives, the Church receives, and through this exchange of love, new members are brought into the **invisible** covenant with God.

THE UNIVERSAL CATHOLIC FAMILY

Jesus

New Members

Everyday Participation

To be Catholic means participating in God's eternal, hidden mystery of union and communion. This is His master plan for our lives. But what does it mean to "participate" in God's inner mystery of love?

Think about how you participate in things on Earth: playing a musical instrument in a band, laughing with your friends, joining the track team or debate club, discussing literature in school, or spending time with your family. When you participate, you actively enter into a relationship or undertaking.

Tim, John Paul, and Michael played on the football team together since 9th grade. At first, they mostly sat the bench, but as they became better football players, they contributed more to the team. As seniors, their participation helped their team, the Lumberjacks, to win the state championship.

Participation in God's Inner Life of Love

Anyone who loves—who really gives the gift of self—participates in God's eternal mystery. So when you give your teacher the gift of your attention, receive your mom's care when you are sick, or play soccer with your friends, you are participating in God's eternal exchange of love.

An important way to participate in God's master plan is through family life. A family is a sign of God's faithful, covenantal union with each person.

Matt, Theresa, and Logan used to hate folding clean clothes and always argued about whose chore it was. But one evening, they were in a hurry to attend the school play, and all three of them pitched in. They were surprised at how quickly the work got done. From then on, they always folded the clothes together and had great fun. They participated in family life.

"And this is the mystery of Truth and Love, the mystery of divine life, in which [each human] really participates."

Theology of the Body 19:4

"As the Father loves me, so I also love you. Remain in my love."
—Jn. 15:9

"Only if I serve my neighbor can my eyes be opened to what God does for me and how much He loves me."
—Pope Benedict XVI
Benedictus

© Copyright 2019 by Monica Ashour. All rights reserved.

11

Covenant Matters

You might be thinking, *"Wait! My family life is a participation in God's master plan?! But we're not perfect. We've got some real problems."* It is true that real families have fights and failures, breakdowns and break-ups. Like Adam and Eve, people do not always remain true to their covenants. Sin and frailties can harm even a seemingly perfect family.

Instead of studying the distortions of the family, we must recognize the good that God intends through families. It would not be fair to base your opinion of apples on a single sour one, would it? Instead, you should take a good apple as your example. Use the same criterion for learning about family. Healthy family life is characterized by closeness, laughter, love, and a great deal of forgiveness.

When families are healthy and functioning well, the covenant of marriage is the best natural sign of God's own covenant with us in Jesus Christ. Why? Because it is an example of participation in the union and communion of life-giving love. It is an example of the Gospel.

Mirror, Mirror on the Wall

Think of marriage as a mirror. When marriage is misunderstood, the image of Christ and His Church becomes warped, like in a funhouse mirror at a carnival. The truth is distorted. However, as in the graphic below, a strong marriage and family reflect a very clear image of Christ and His Church.

© Copyright 2019 by Monica Ashour. All rights reserved.

This, of course, does not mean everyone gets married (there are priests, religious, and singles), but marriage serves as a visible sign that we are all meant to be in family and friendship and fellowship.

Do you see why marriage is so important in Catholic theology? It reveals the pattern of God's fruitful covenant of life and love carried out all over the world.

So...
the more we understand the truth of the **body**,
the more we understand the truth of **marriage**;
and the more we understand the truth of **marriage**,
the more we understand **Catholicism**;
and the more we understand **Catholicism**,
the more we understand **God Himself**!

Points to Ponder:
1. What are some ways you participate with others? What gifts do you bring to each activity?
2. What is God's inner mystery? How can you participate in God's mystery?

Mission: For the rest of this week, be aware of how you live in union and communion with your classmates, team, and family. Then, at Mass on Sunday, offer thanks to God for all the people who participate in your life.

Sacraments EmBODY Covenant

Hidden Reality

Have you and your friends ever invented a fun handshake? Or exchanged friendship bracelets? The handshake and the bracelets are symbols of loyalty and belonging. They are visible signs representing your friendship.

God also works through visible signs. God invites each of us into covenant through His Church, and the visible signs He offers to us are the sacraments: Baptism, Eucharist, Confirmation, Reconciliation, Anointing of the Sick, Holy Orders, and Matrimony.

Just like the covenants in salvation history, the sacraments are encounters with God. A sacrament is a visible sign which points to and brings about a supernatural, invisible reality.

God knows we are "body-persons," and as such, He knows we need tangible signs of His love. Every time we receive a sacrament, we are invited to deeper friendship with God through Jesus Christ.

"...[The sacrament] always 'makes visible' the supernatural mystery that is at work...."
Theology of the Body 93:5

The Catholic Perspective

Catholics have a sacramental view of reality. That means that the things we cannot see are just as important as the things we can see. For example, we know that courage exists, even though it is invisible. The Theology of the Body, with its emphasis on the whole person, takes both the visible and invisible seriously.

What if a friend thinks she can ace her math class alone, without God's grace? Yet she has a God-given intellect; we can do nothing without God. Now suppose another friend makes an A in math, but he tells you, "I had nothing to do with it; it was all God!" That sounds very pious, but is that true? All we have to do is pray? No studying necessary? Both of these friends are only half right.

To focus **only** on what is earthly and natural is to forget divinity. This mistake is called *secularism*. Conversely, if the focus is **only** on supernatural things, it is easy to forget the importance of nature and the body. This is called *over-spiritualizing*.

So, a boy who works out all the time and only focuses on his physical health, ignoring his spiritual needs, falls into secularism.

Catholics Choose Both!

Natural		Supernatural
Visible		Invisible
Body		Spirit
Reason	AND!	Faith
Earth		Heaven
Time		Eternity
Human		Divine

Based on Dr. Mark Lowery's chart "The Catholic Ands." Used with permission. © Copyright 2019 by Monica Ashour. All rights reserved.

On the other hand, a girl on the softball team who simply prays to hit a home run without practicing her swing, falls into over-spiritualizing the game.

Both views contradict the Catholic, sacramental view of reality wherein we are active players in the drama of life. God works through and with us. We study **and** pray. We go to basketball games **and** go to Mass. Catholicism chooses both the visible **and** invisible, especially because of Jesus Christ, Who is both man **and** God.

Matter Matters in the Sacraments

God prefers to reach us through matter. Can we receive the sacraments without our bodies? No. It is through our bodies (visible) that God inhabits our souls (invisible).

José has racked up a number of sins—he has lost his temper with his family, and he has allowed lust to enter his heart. He's feeling really bad about it all, and he knows that he needs to repair his friendship with God. The next day, he makes his confession and hears these words from the priest: "Through the ministry of the Church, may God give you pardon and peace. And I absolve you of your sins, in the name of the Father and of the Son and of the Holy Spirit." His heart lightens as he heads out to do his act of penance. Body and spirit, he has encountered God in Confession.

Anna is struggling with her faith. She feels alone in the world, and it seems as though all of her friends are fake. She's also worried about her cousin in the hospital. At Sunday Mass, as she approaches Holy Communion, she prays: "Jesus, help me!" When she receives the sacred Body and precious Blood of Our Lord, she does not feel anything different emotionally, but she knows—in a real and tangible way—that she is not alone. God loves her. Body and spirit, she has encountered God in the Eucharist.

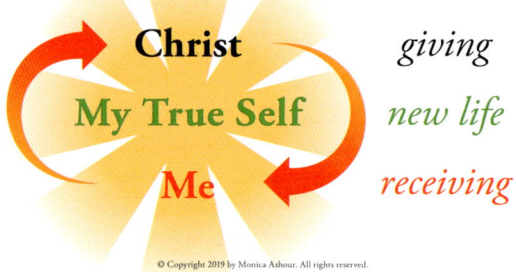

"For in him were created all things in heaven and on earth, the visible and the invisible...."
Col. 1:16

The Sacraments are Gifts from God through the Church

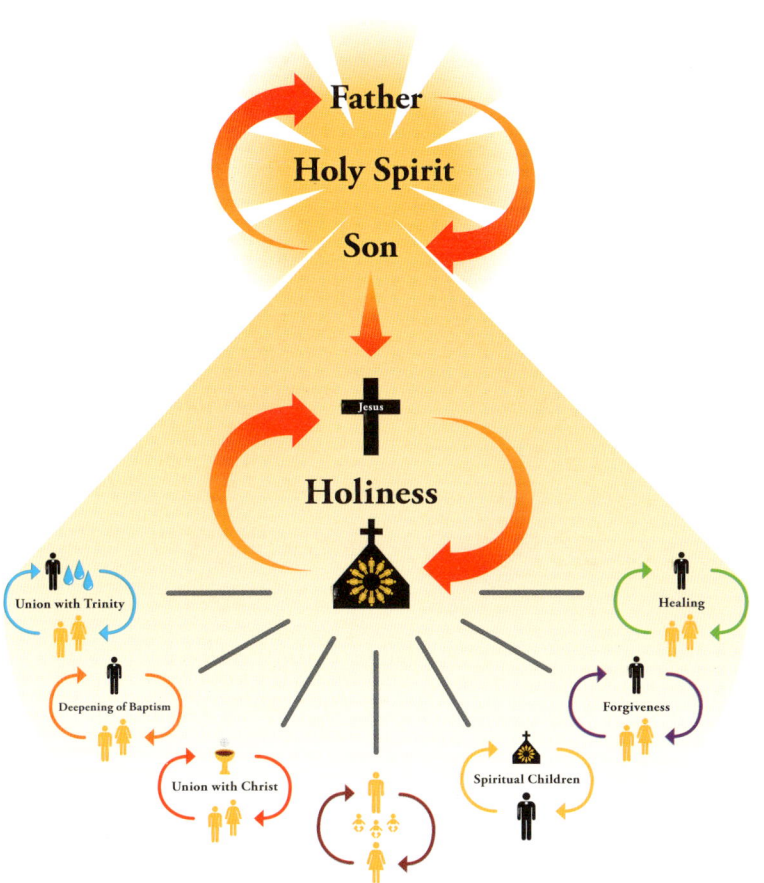

A Person-to-Person Encounter

A sacrament is not a thing that you receive. You actually receive someBODY—Jesus Himself. You encounter a living Person, not a thing.

When you "receive grace" in the sacraments, it means that the Blessed Trinity is sharing divine life and love with you. The veil between time and eternity is pulled back for a moment, and you are united with God. This strengthens you to become your authentic self because you are growing in holiness.

Each time you celebrate the sacraments, you renew your covenant with God which began at Baptism. In each sacrament, Jesus gives Himself to you, and you offer yourself to Him. This exchange of love allows you to radiate His grace to others.

The Key to Grace

Each sacrament brings forth a supernatural reality and new life, for it is an encounter with Christ.

Sacrament	Supernatural Reality	New Life
Baptism	union & communion with the Trinity	child of God who brings others to Christ
Eucharist	union & communion with the Body of Christ	sanctified to love others
Holy Orders	given power to stand *in persona Christi*	given charism to teach, govern, and sanctify
Reconciliation	forgiveness of sin; freedom to love	spiritual healing; deeper union with Christ's Body
Confirmation	baptismal vocation sealed	empowered to carry out one's baptismal mission
Anointing of the Sick	strength to carry one's cross with Christ	healing and fortitude
Marriage	spousal bond participating in God	supernatural grace & natural children

© Copyright 2019 by Monica Ashour. All rights reserved.

St. John Paul calls marriage a "weight-bearing structure" for all of the sacraments, for it is the best natural sign of the covenant established by Christ and His Bride, the Church.

"...[M]arriage constitutes...the underlying, weight-bearing structure of... the sacramental order...." *Theology of the Body 98:2*

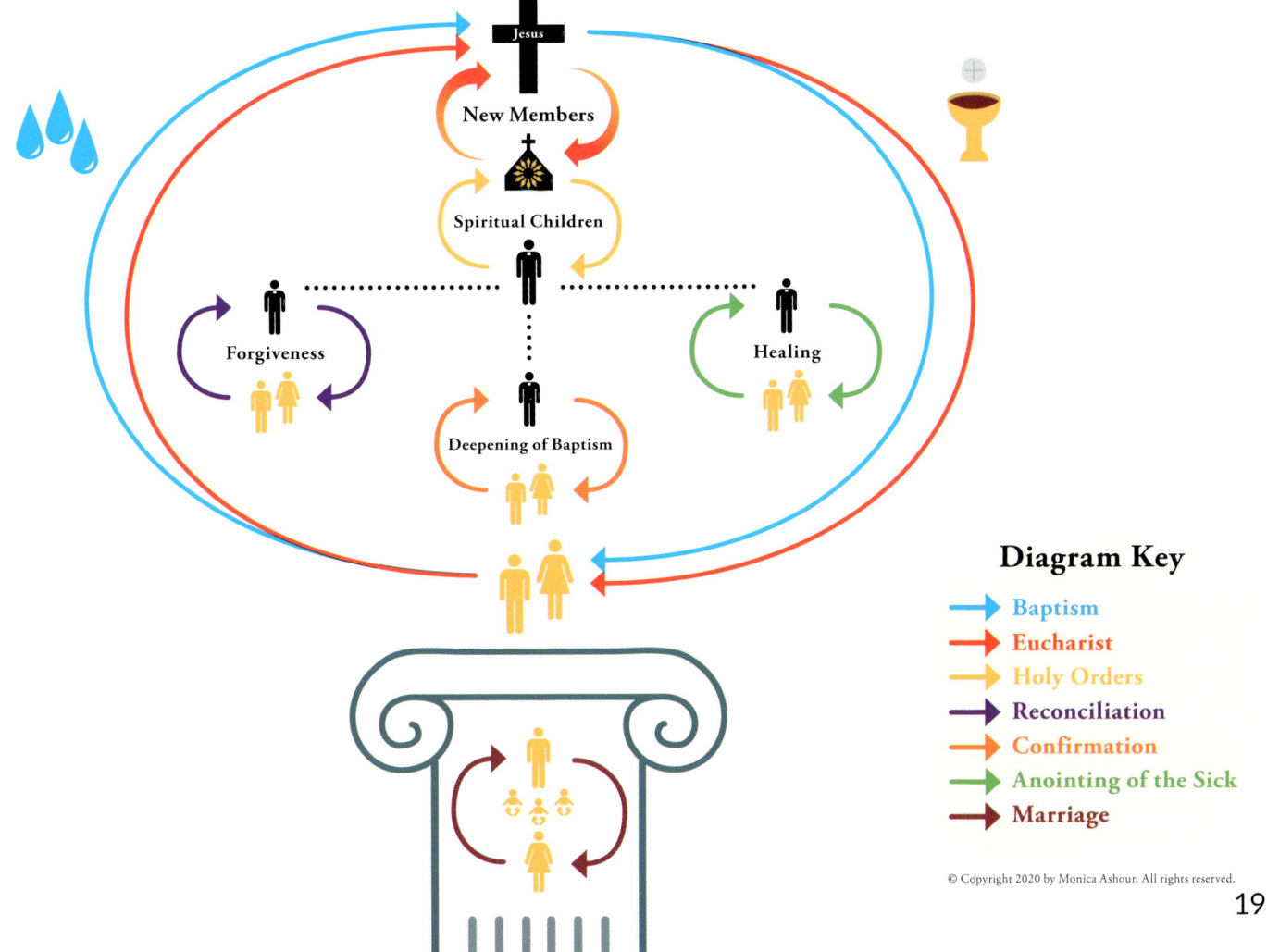

Bearing the Weight of the World

What does St. John Paul mean when he calls marriage the "weight-bearing structure" for all of the sacraments? Consider this analogy. Marriage is like Atlas, the Titan from Greek mythology. In the myth, Atlas holds the weight of the heavens and Earth upon his shoulders, keeping everything balanced and stable. Likewise, our understanding of all the sacraments is balanced and supported by the Sacrament of Marriage.

But what if Atlas were to grow weary? The heavens and Earth would come crashing down. Similarly, when marriage becomes more distorted and undervalued, our understanding of all the sacraments and Catholicism itself comes crashing down.

A solid (if imperfect) marriage tells the world, "Through good times and bad, we as a family are covenanted together." Similarly, the sacraments are like God and His people saying, "Through good times and bad, we as a Catholic family are covenanted together."

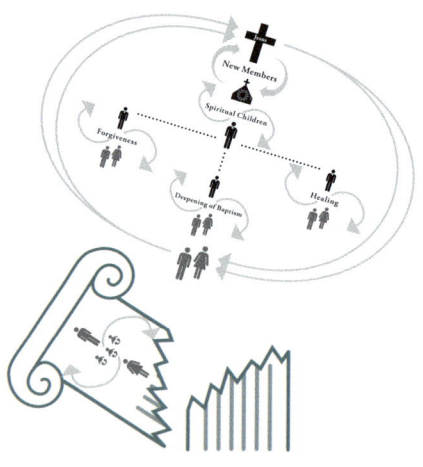

© Copyright 2019 by Monica Ashour. All rights reserved.

Seeing the parallels between marriage and the other sacraments helps us understand Catholicism better. Let's focus on three patterns in a strong marriage that are also present in the sacraments:
- giving-receiving-new life;
- same nature-union-new life;
- free-full-faithful-fruitful.

"...[A]ll the sacraments of the New Covenant find their prototype in some way in marriage as the primordial sacrament."

Theology of the Body 98:2

20

 "...[A sacrament] is 'a visible sign of an invisible reality,' [and in] this sign—God gives himself to [us]...." *Theology of the Body 87:5*

Marriage

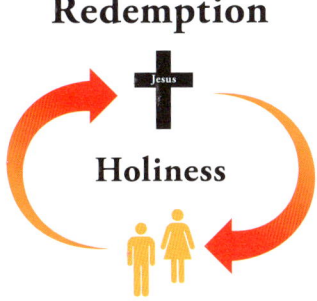

Redemption

Marriage: Giving-Receiving-New Life

Imagine going to a wedding, and when the priest asks the couple if they will love and honor each other for as long as they both shall live, they respond, "No, only when we feel like it." Would that surprise you? Why? It's because you know that whether they feel like it or not, the couple is meant to love each other and to live out their covenant by **giving** and **receiving**. The more open they are to each other, the closer they will be. Their faithful choice to love yields a joyful **life**, even in hard times.

Sacraments: Giving-Receiving-New Life

Jesus loves and honors you by being present in the sacraments. And you love and honor Him by receiving the sacraments as long as you shall live. Whether you feel like it or not, you can live out this covenant with Christ by **giving** and **receiving**. Of course, the more open you are to His grace, the more He can dwell within you. Love is based in the will, and staying true to Christ gives you a joyful **life**, even in hard times.

21

Marriage: Same Nature, Union, New Life

Have you ever been to a wedding where a man was marrying a shark? Or a woman was marrying a teddy bear? No? Why not? Those who marry must have the **same nature**—human nature. Only those of the same nature can have real union and create new life together.

Would you expect to be invited to the wedding of a person who wants to marry himself or herself? No? Why not? Marriage is about **union**. It involves two people of the same nature, a husband and a wife, who complement each other. They share hopes, dreams, a home, faith—everything.

Could you imagine a man and woman who decide to spend the rest of their lives alone, in total isolation without anyone else, because they are so "in love"? No? Why not?

Love is meant to bring **new life** to the world. Love is meant to overflow to others and to help them in their journey toward Heaven.

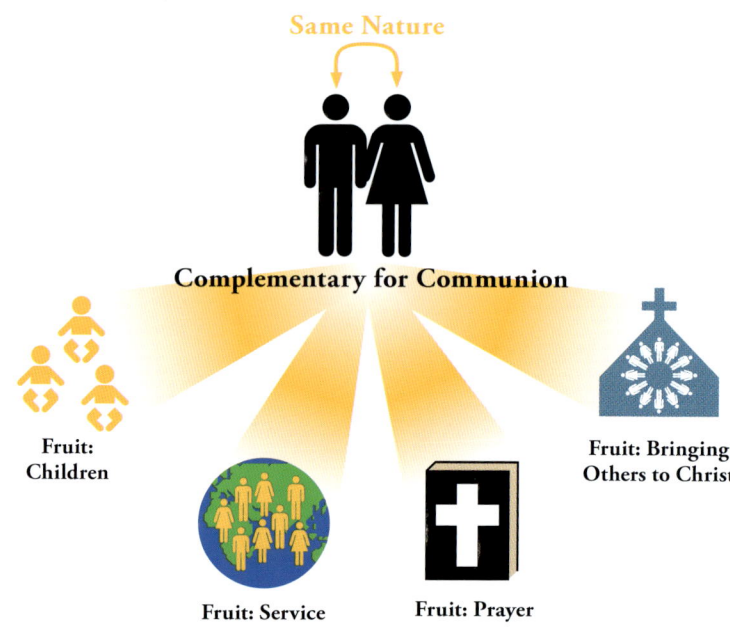

Sacraments of Initiation

Baptism
Same Nature

Eucharist
Union

Confirmation
New Life

© Copyright 2019 by Monica Ashour. All rights reserved.

"Through [His divine power], you may come to share in the divine nature...."
2 Pt. 1:4

Sacraments: Same Nature, Union, New Life

You are human, and God is divine. You can't be in a covenantal union with God if you don't share His nature. Yet, God shares His **divine nature** with us through Baptism. You become God's child in a very real sense through the visible sign of water poured on your head.

Which sacrament provides the greatest union with God? The Eucharist. In this Bread of Life, Jesus allows us not only the closest **union** with Him, but communion with the Church around the world, as well as those in Purgatory and in Heaven.

The Sacrament of Confirmation demonstrates that you are ready to bring **new life** to others, for to be Christian is to be a "little Christ." When you give the gift of self, you draw others to Christ and help them on their way to Heaven.

It is no accident that these three sacraments parallel marriage. St. John Paul gave us the Theology of the Body to preserve the sacredness of Matrimony, which reminds us that we are all called to participate in the eternal covenant of union and communion with God, renewed through the sacraments.

Marriage: Free, Full, Faithful, Fruitful

One final way to gain a better understanding of the sacraments is to look at the four foundational attributes of marriage: **free**, **full**, **faithful**, and **fruitful**.

Would it be good if spouses were forced to marry each other against their will? No? Why not? It should be a free choice. Covenantal love is **free**.

Could you imagine a wedding where the bride said to her groom: "I give you my time, my faithfulness, my fertility, but not my heart." No? Why not? Husbands and wives share everything with each other. Covenantal love is **full**.

Would you expect to be invited to the wedding of one man to several women? No? Why not? Marriage means choosing one spouse to love and cherish until death. Covenantal love is **faithful**.

Have you been to a wedding where the priest says to the couple, "Will you accept children lovingly from God…" and the couple declines, saying, "We are not open to children." No? Why not? Children are a sign of new life. Covenantal love is **fruitful**.

Sacraments: Free, Full, Faithful, Fruitful

Isn't it fascinating that the four attributes that characterize marriage should also characterize our life in Christ?

Can you ever be forced to receive a sacrament? Of course not. It is your **free** decision to encounter Christ, and He gives Himself freely to you.

God pours Himself out for you, and, in turn, He asks for your whole life, not just part of you. God wants you to share everything with Him, now and eternally. Receiving the sacraments with an open heart is giving Him your **full** self.

In the first Commandment, God asks you to worship Him alone. How can you obey that command? In receiving the sacraments, you are worshipping God and showing Him that you are in covenant with Him. God wants you to be **faithful** to Him.

The sacraments draw you close to Jesus and fill you with His grace; then, you are empowered to love. The sacraments bring you new life and make you **fruitful** in your Christian covenant.

Free
Full
Faithful
Fruitful

Getting Marriage Right

Are you surprised to learn that a proper understanding of marriage leads to a richer appreciation of our Catholic Faith? The pattern of marriage is reflected in all of the sacraments. Why? Because it is the pattern of love.
- Love is giving-receiving-new life.
- Love is based on the same nature-union-new life.
- Love is free-full-faithful-fruitful.

No wonder marriage is seen as a pillar, which holds up the truth of love.

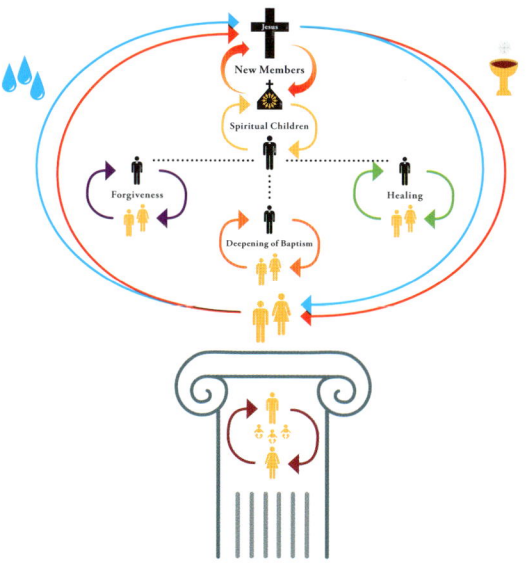

Points to Ponder:
1. How can you be more mindful of your encounter with Christ in the sacraments?
2. Name some specific ways this Theology of the Body approach to the sacraments helps you to understand your Catholic Faith in a different way.

Mission:
Think about a family that you admire, and write down their attributes. Choose one of those attributes and live it out intentionally in your personal relationship with Christ and His Church.

3 The Body as Prophet

Prophets Speak for God

Prophets proclaim God's covenants. Think of the Old Testament prophets you know, like Elijah, Isaiah, Ezekiel, and Jonah. They were rarely popular when they were alive, but they had an important mission that made them unforgettable: they delivered the news of God's covenant to His people.

A prophet serves as the conscience of the people. For their own good, he reminds them again and again to keep their covenant with God.

Yet even before the prophets, an understanding of covenant has always been part of human nature. How do we know? Because God gave us bodies. How is the body a sign of covenant?

Our bodies are made for union and communion; they reveal the nature of God. In other words, as St. John Paul points out, the body is a prophet.

"By participating in the eternal plan of Love,... [the mystery hidden in God], the 'language of the body' becomes in fact a 'prophetism of the body'...."
Theology of the Body 123:2

The Body Speaks for God

Consider Adam, the very first human. He named the animals and enjoyed all the fruits of Eden, but something was lacking. Adam's body, like a prophet, told him that he was meant to be a gift. Adam wanted to give, but there was noBODY of the same nature to receive his gift.

For the first time in the Bible, God declared that something was wrong: "It is not good for the man to be alone" (Gen. 2:18). And so God made Eve. He designed man and woman to complement each other, and He taught them this through their bodies. Adam and Eve were prophets to each other, giving and receiving the message of fruitful love.

St. John Paul points out that all people—not just married people—are meant to give and receive the message of love. We can hug each other and walk together; we can play sports with our friends and laugh until we cry. The message is repeated over and over again through our bodies: we are made for covenantal love.

We proclaim love by the gift of self.

When we love, we image God the most.

We are gifts to each other.

The Body Proclaims Love

So, when anyBODY loves sacrificially, generously, and forgivingly, that person is, in a sense, a prophet. St. John Paul teaches that when we give a "gift of self" with our bodily actions, we proclaim, like a prophet, that God is love.

Being a prophet sometimes looks like this:
- You help your sister with her Spanish homework when she is frustrated.
- At lunch, you sit with the classmate that no one else will sit next to.
- You forgive your friend when he lets you down.

A prophet proclaims God's message.

God's main message is Love.

Therefore, a prophet proclaims love.

The body is meant to proclaim love.

Therefore, the body is a prophet.

"A 'prophet' is one who...speaks [God's] truth in the place of God, in his name and in some sense with his authority."
Theology of the Body 105:2

You Can Be a Prophet

It is not easy being a prophet; just look at history. People often reject prophets and their messages from God because they do not like to be confronted with their own sins.

Prophets have always been persecuted for speaking the truth. Amos was rejected by his people, Daniel was thrown into a den of lions, Jeremiah was dropped into a pit, and Zechariah was stoned, just to name a few. No wonder Jonah ran and hid from God when he was asked to deliver a message from the Lord!

As prophets, we need to be both brave and persistent. We all generally tend toward the path of least resistance because accepting sin sometimes seems to be the easiest thing to do. In the end, though, sin is always harmful. In fact, sin diminishes who you are, making you, in a sense, less than yourself—a "false prophet," you might say.

Notice in the chart below that the left column shows the easy way out, and the right column shows faithfulness to God's covenant. Are you strong enough to be a true prophet for others?

False Prophet	True Prophet
Disobeying your parents in front of your younger siblings.	Choosing to obey your parents and helping your siblings to see the peace it brings.
Taking part in online bullying.	Choosing to stand up for those who are bullied, even if it means you'll be ridiculed.
Not saying anything about impure videos.	Choosing to speak up for what is wholesome.
Giving in to lust.	Choosing to deny selfish desires.

© Copyright 2019 by Monica Ashour. All rights reserved.

Married Couples as Prophets

Married couples are prophets to each other. At their wedding, a man and a woman express their vows through the language of words. However, their marriage is not a full reality until their bodies, like prophets, speak the language of married love. In that sacred act, the couple is bonded for life.

In their time together on Earth, the couple's covenantal bond is unbreakable because it is designed by God to participate in and reflect the permanent, covenantal bond of Jesus and the Church. St. John Paul says that a husband and wife are true prophets to each other when their love is free, full, faithful, and fruitful.

Prophets in Word and in Body

Visible Sign	Invisible Reality
Language of Words Man and woman **exchange vows** that are free, full, faithful, and fruitful.	Each **freely consents** to enter into marriage to help each other get to Heaven and to live for the other.
Language of the Body The male body and female body come together in a **marital union** that is free, full, faithful, and fruitful.	**The spouses are bonded for life** and are meant to participate in the eternal, fruitful covenant of Christ and the Church.

© Copyright 2019 by Monica Ashour. All rights reserved.

Beware of False Prophets

False prophets say that anything goes in the area of sexuality. However, that often leads to broken hearts and damaged bodies. God offers forgiveness and healing to those who have been affected by sin and wish to repair their covenant with Him. They can start anew and live as true prophets according to God's design of the body. All of us are called to be faithful to God's plan for sexuality.

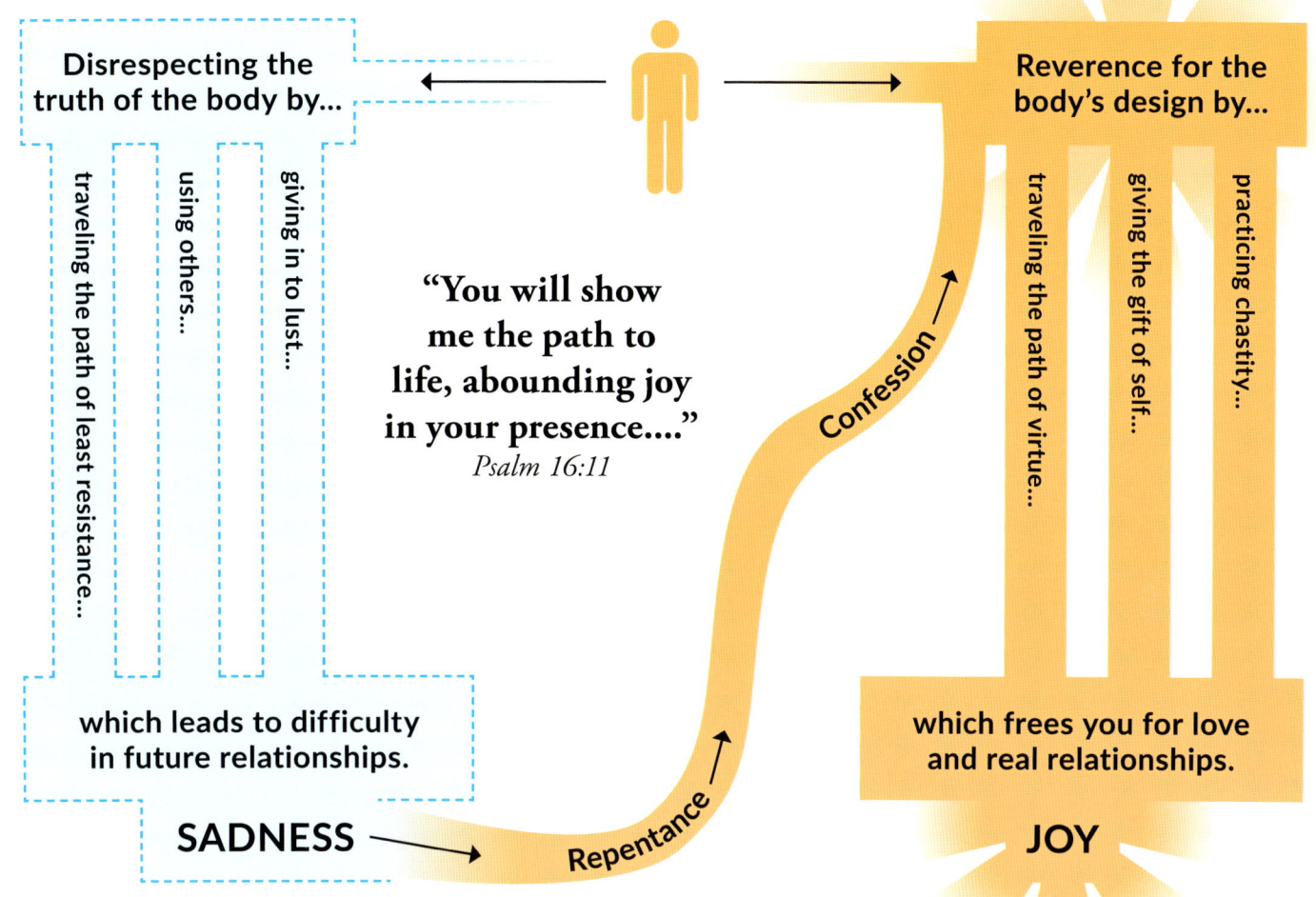

Detachment Divides

Are there obstacles in your calling to be a prophet of truth and love? Every day, whether you know it or not, you are bombarded with messages from false prophets. Mainstream media exposes people to harmful images and situations which often promote extramarital sex, objectification of women, violence, vulgarity, and other behaviors that contradict the dignity of the human person.

When experienced again and again, all of these messages can gradually lead to an acceptance of sin, which, in turn, leads to what St. John Paul calls "detachment." Detached means disconnected. People who fall into detachment live as if their bodies are disconnected from any deeper meaning. The result is sadness and brokenness.

Yet, God designed humans to be whole, body and spirit connected. Our bodies should proclaim, like prophets, *I am a gift, and you are a gift*. The result is joy.

"And the Word became flesh...." Jn. 1:14

Detachment
I am cruel to my family.
I talk about myself only.
I experience division.

Reverence
I seek ways to love my family.
I listen to others speak.
I experience communion.

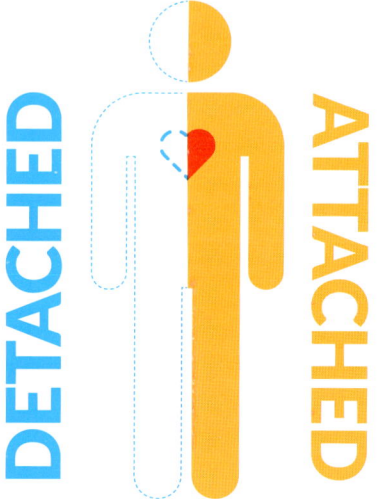

© Copyright 2019 by Monica Ashour. All rights reserved.

"The flesh is the hinge of salvation." CCC 1015

Disregarding Science:
I sever healthy limbs.
I disrupt healthy systems.
I prefer a quick fix.

Respecting Science:
I do no harm.
I respect the natural functions of the body.
I treat the problem at its source.

© Copyright 2019 by Monica Ashour. All rights reserved.

Science Respects the Body

Scientists who study biology have a real grasp of the design of the human person. Unfortunately, some people do not take science seriously. They say, "It's my body; I can do whatever I want with it." This may seem reasonable at first, but is it?

Let's follow this idea to its logical conclusion with an extreme example. Suppose a friend of yours felt like her body was out of order and so she wanted to surgically swap her arms and her legs. Would a doctor be helping your friend by doing this surgery? Science and medicine are not meant to **harm** a perfectly functioning body, but to **heal** an injured or diseased body to bring it back to health. A doctor who respects the body's design respects both science and the patients themselves.

A false prophet may say, "Whatever works for you; why should I care?" This response not only ignores science, but it also avoids the responsibility to speak truth in love. False prophets diminish the truth of the body and so ultimately diminish God's message of love.

33

The Body Is a Gift to be Received

St. John Paul teaches that the body is a gift from God that reveals the whole person. However, some ideas are detached from that objective truth. They place feelings above the science of the body. As shown in the diagram below, people experience detachment in different ways. However, each of us is to receive all of creation as a gift. The body is a prophet whose message is love and communion.

Consider these examples:
- What if an adult decides he is six years old? Should he be allowed in first grade?
- What if a six year old feels like she is sixteen? Should she be given a driver's license?
- What if a twenty-five year old man decides he is a high school girl? Should he be allowed to compete at the girls' state track meet and win all the races?

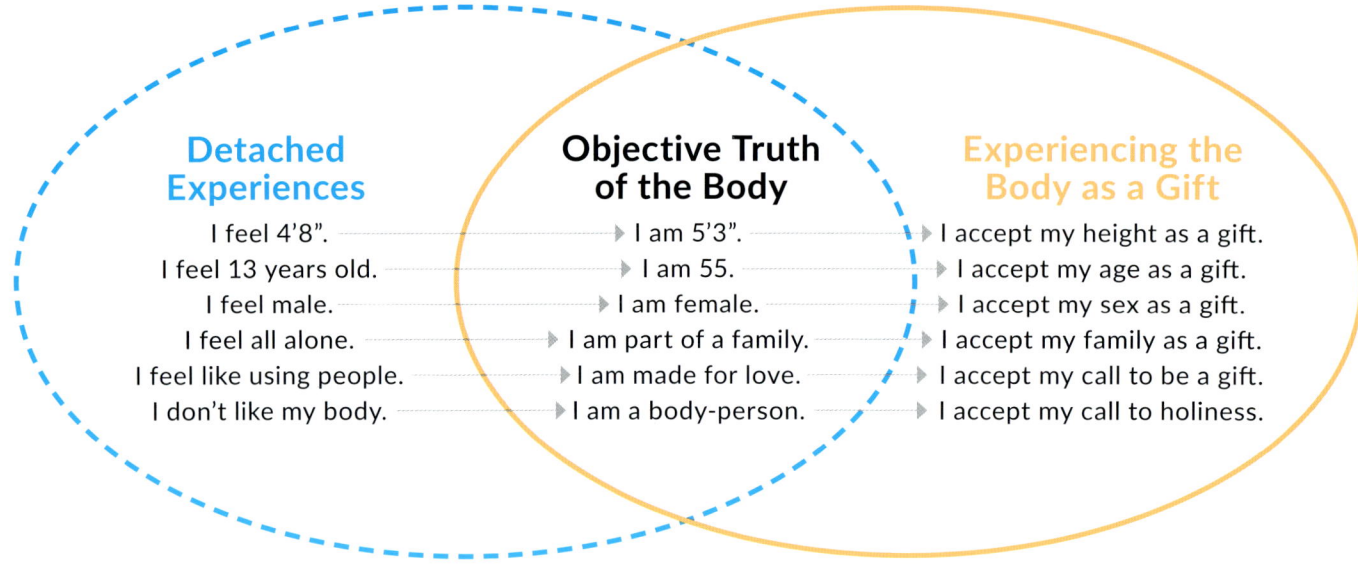

© Copyright 2019 by Monica Ashour. All rights reserved.

The Church Stands Up for EveryBODY

Detachment affects the decisions people make and the messages we hear. False prophets who preach detachment can be compelling, but as Jesus Himself warned us, "Beware of false prophets, who come to you in sheep's clothing, but underneath are ravenous wolves" (Mt. 7:15). So, where can we find the truth?

God not only designs our bodies to be prophets, but He has given us a Body that is a prophet for the whole world—His own Mystical Body, the Church. The Church stands up for the truth. The Church stands up for the body. The Church stands up for love. **Every single teaching** of the Catholic Church is meant to help everyBODY. The various teachings of the Catholic Church are cohesive, like a beautifully woven tapestry.

It's All About Love

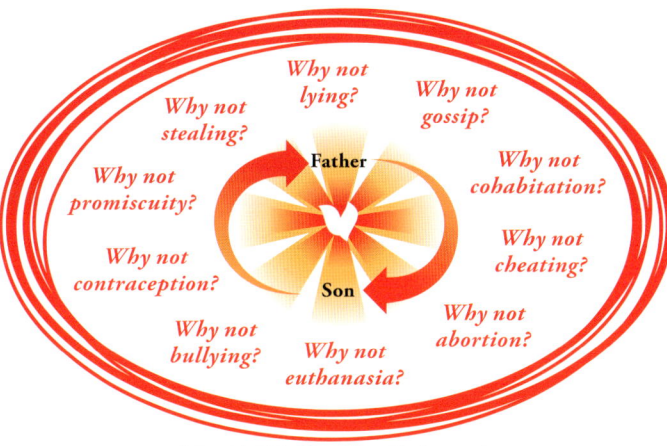

© Copyright 2019 by Monica Ashour. All rights reserved.

When false prophets disagree with certain teachings, it is as if they are pulling out single threads, which unravels the tapestry of truth and distorts its beauty. Catholicism is consistent, because love is consistent.

"We believe in God who is creator of the flesh; we believe in the Word made flesh in order to redeem the flesh; we believe in the resurrection of the flesh, the fulfillment of both the creation and the redemption of the flesh."

CCC 1015

The Church Helping Those in Need

The Church cares for the whole person; She does not detach body from spirit. You will notice below that both physical and spiritual needs are provided for in the Body of Christ.

These are called the Corporal (Bodily) and the Spiritual Works of Mercy. You can be a prophet when you give the gift of self in the works of mercy.

The Works of Mercy

For Physical Needs
- Ransom the captive
- Visit the sick and imprisoned
- Feed the hungry
- Bury the dead
- Shelter the homeless
- Give drink to the thirsty
- Clothe the naked

For Spiritual Needs
- Comfort the afflicted
- Counsel the doubtful
- Admonish the sinner
- Pray for the living and the dead
- Instruct the ignorant
- Bear wrongs patiently
- Forgive injuries

"And whoever gives [even] a cup of cold water to one of these little ones to drink because he is a disciple—amen, I say to you, he will surely not lose his reward." Mt. 10:42

> "[The body is] the transparent sign of interpersonal 'communion'...."
> *Theology of the Body 59:2*

The Body as Prophet of God's Love

St. John Paul's Theology of the Body is a powerful message about the truth and meaning of the body, particularly about God's gift of human sexuality. God designed the human person—body and spirit—to experience true love.

Detachment detracts from the design of love. Detachment does not take the science of the body seriously. Detachment does not honor the body's Designer or reverence the body. Your body is a prophet when you live the truth of covenantal love.

Points to Ponder:
1. How do you prophesy with your body at home, at school, and other places?
2. What is the relationship between science and religion? How do the two complement each other?

Mission: For the rest of the week, notice any "False Prophets" you see and hear in the media. Discuss their messages with your parents.

4 The Center of Catholicism

The Sign of the Cross

If you were to draw a symbol to represent *covenant*, what would you draw? Would you make a circle because it has no beginning and no end? Or perhaps you'd draw a line since it extends infinitely in both directions. Maybe a triangle, since it's recognized by architects to be the strongest shape. But perhaps the best symbol would be a cross. Why?

Pope Benedict calls the cross the "center of reality." Notice that the vertical line of the cross connects Heaven to Earth. The arms of the cross, though, connect and embrace all that is in the world. In other words, the simple, two-lined shape of the cross is a message, and it's the message Jesus called the greatest commandment: love God and love your neighbor. The cross is a sign of love, a sign of covenant. And Whom do we find at the center of the cross, at the intersection of God and man? Jesus.

Mass: The Greatest Union

UNION — UNION WITH OTHERS — GOD

© Copyright 2019 by Monica Ashour. All rights reserved.

The Sign of the New and Eternal Covenant

What is the significance of the crucifix? Why do we see Jesus' Body on the cross when we know that He rose from the dead? It's because His Body matters. The crucified Body of Jesus is where the past and the future meet. It is where God is glorified, and we are made holy. This is the mystery of the Mass.

At Mass, we enter a sort of "time warp." First, we go back in time to Jerusalem. We experience a re-presentation of the Last Supper, as well as Jesus' sacrificial Gift of Self on Calvary. That's why it is called the Holy Sacrifice of the Mass. This "time warp" also propels us forward into the eternity of Heaven. We are in union and communion with God and all of the saints. This is why Scripture calls the Mass the "Supper of the Lamb" (Rev. 19:7-10), for it is a great, eternal feast.

Jesus' Body on the cross transcends time and space, and reaches us here and now.

The Eternal Covenant Fulfilled at Mass

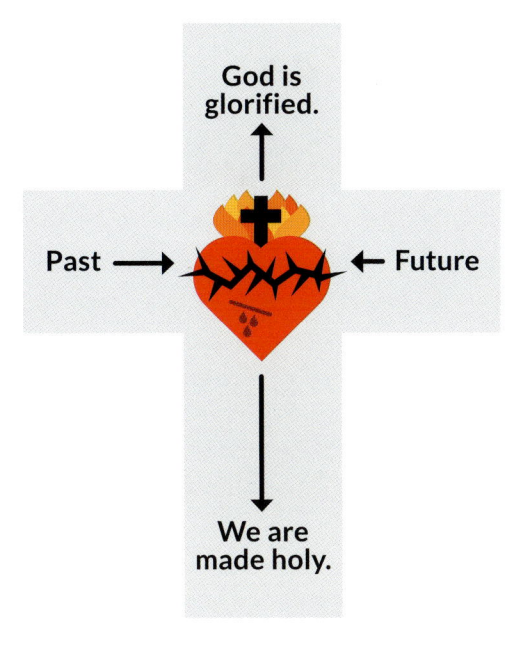

God is glorified.
Past → ← Future
We are made holy.

© Copyright 2019 by Monica Ashour. All rights reserved.

"Apart from the cross there is no other ladder by which we may get to heaven." *CCC 618*

The Solitude of the Cross

Christ's crucifixion involved every kind of suffering—physical, mental, emotional, and spiritual. It is a paradox that, in order to bring us into union with His Father, Jesus Himself had to suffer a total loss of union. He experienced the extremes of isolation before His death.

On the cross Jesus was completely alone. He belonged neither to Heaven nor Earth. His Body hung between them, in a no-man's land.

The world rejected Jesus. His friends abandoned Him... He was mocked and spat upon... He even let go of His own mother... and He cried out to His Father in Heaven, "My God, my God, why hast thou forsaken me?" (Mt. 27:46).

Jesus knew total isolation. Why? For you.

This is the mystery of the cross. Out of love for us, Jesus chose to experience this isolation to save us from eternal isolation. In other words, His was an experience of Hell.

What is Hell? Ultimate loneliness. Ultimate isolation. No communion—the opposite of God's plan for us.

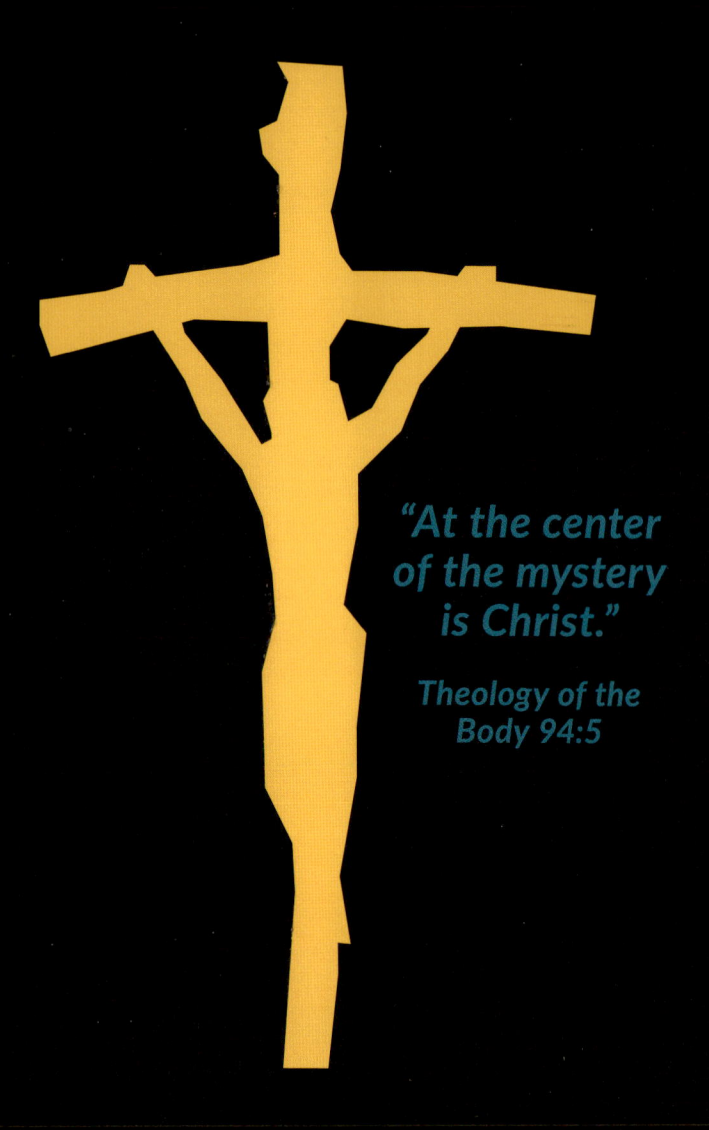

"At the center of the mystery is Christ."

Theology of the Body 94:5

Holy Saturday: No-Body Around

The isolation of Good Friday extends further. Holy Saturday is the only day of the year we cannot receive the Body of Christ. Why? On Holy Saturday, Christ descended into Hell while His sacred Body lay in the tomb. Because Jesus' human soul was separated from His Body, we too, in our commemoration of Holy Saturday, are separated from His Body.

This is the mystery of Holy Saturday. This is the day tabernacles throughout the world are empty. This is the day there is no Liturgy. This is the day no one receives the Body of Christ. Without Holy Mass, we wait, recalling Jesus' death. Because Catholicism takes the body so seriously, when the Church says we cannot receive the Body of Christ, there must be a serious reason.

The Church wants us to meditate on life without the Eucharist. This teaches us to long for Eucharistic union and communion with Our Lord.

> "Jesus Christ, by remaining in death, passed beyond the door of this ultimate solitude.... [T]his is exactly what happened on Holy Saturday: the voice of God resounded in the realm of death. The unimaginable occurred: namely, Love penetrated 'hell.'"
> —Pope Benedict XVI
> *Meditation on the Veneration of the Holy Shroud*

"'By the grace of God' Jesus tasted death 'for every one'. In his plan of salvation, God ordained that his Son should not only 'die for our sins' but should also 'taste death', experience the condition of death, the separation of his soul from his body, between the time he expired on the cross and the time he was raised from the dead. The state of the dead Christ is the mystery of the tomb and the descent into hell. It is the mystery of Holy Saturday...." CCC 624

The Suspense of the Easter Vigil

The Paschal Mystery—the life, death, and resurrection of Jesus—continues into the Easter Vigil. This is the Mass *par excellence*, which begins in the total darkness of Holy Saturday. The Church meets outside at night.

The suspense builds.

Then… a spark from the Paschal candle. A sign of hope. A sign of resurrection. Led by the light of the Paschal candle, members of the congregation process into the dark sanctuary, which symbolizes the darkness of Christ's tomb.

The suspense builds.

In darkness, seven readings from the Old Testament proclaim the story of salvation and the covenants of God with His people. The Messiah has not yet come.

The suspense builds.

The Risen Body

Suddenly, light floods the church, bells ring out, incense perfumes the air, flowers appear, the altar is adorned, and strains of the Alleluia sound through the sanctuary!

The New Testament readings are proclaimed with joy and gladness, for the Church exults in Jesus, Who is the Way to covenantal union and communion with God.

Now that the Liturgy of the Word has been proclaimed, it is time for the Liturgy of the Eucharist. Held in suspense on Holy Saturday, now on the Day of Resurrection we behold the Body of Christ once again on the holy altar and in the sacred tabernacle.

The story of Christ continues today and forever. It does not end with solitude, pain, isolation, or Hell… for Jesus rose from the dead! His Body is glorified. We can share in His Easter victory when we receive Him in Holy Communion at every Mass. Heaven and Earth are reunited in Christ.

Alleluia! He is risen. He is risen indeed!

No Church, No Covenant

Jesus' resurrection is the message of Christianity, for love is stronger than death. This is why Christianity can be described as the wedding of Heaven and Earth. Imagine a wedding where there was only a groom but no bride. You can't have one without the other. In the wedding of Heaven and Earth, Jesus is the Groom, and the Church is His Bride.

> "...[T]he Church lives from the sacrament of redemption and on her part completes this sacrament...."
> *Theology of the Body 97:4*

Adam & Eve

Remember Adam's loneliness in the garden? He was alone in his human nature, so God the Father cast Adam into a deep sleep.

The rib (symbolizing his human nature) taken from Adam's side produces someBODY. She is of his same nature; she is his bride, Eve.

Adam's natural body awakes, and he speaks the words of covenant: "Bone of my bone and flesh of my flesh." Eve receives Adam's gift; together they form the first human covenant, so fruitful it yields all members of the human race.

Jesus & the Church

Remember Jesus' loneliness in the Garden of Gethsemane? He was alone on the cross, and God the Father allowed Jesus to go into the deep "sleep" of death.

The water and blood (symbolizing His human and divine natures) flowing from Christ's side produces someBODY. She is of His dual natures; she is His Bride, the Church.

Jesus' resurrected Body "awakes," and He speaks the words of covenant: "This is My Body, given for you." The Church receives Jesus' Gift; together they form the New and Eternal Covenant, so fruitful it yields all members of the Body of Christ.

No Mary, No Covenant

The covenant between Christ and the Church would not be possible without Mother Mary. At every moment in her life, she lived in covenant with God **freely**, **fully**, **faithfully**, and **fruitfully**. Moreover, the mutual **giving** and **receiving** between God and Mary brought about Christianity when Mary received **new life**—the unborn Body of her Son—in her body. She was the very first Christian to receive Christ bodily, and we follow her example when we receive the Eucharist.

However, Mary was human, and God is divine. Since she is not God and was born before the Sacrament of Baptism was instituted, how could she and God be in union? This is why the Church teaches the truth of the Immaculate Conception—at the very moment of Mary's conception, she participated in the **same nature** as God: divine nature. Therefore, she could be in **union** with God the Holy Spirit and bear the **fruit** of her womb, Jesus. This is why Catholics honor Mary and call her Queen of Heaven and Earth.

The Incarnation: The Word Made Flesh

Holy Spirit
Giver of Divine Life

Jesus
Incarnate Son of God

Mary
Participating in Divinity

giving

fruit

receiving

"The holy Spirit will come upon you, and the power of the Most High will overshadow you. Therefore the child to be born will be called holy, the Son of God." — Luke 1:35

© Copyright 2019 by Monica Ashour. All rights reserved.

Cosmic Catholicism

Through the cross, the entire cosmos is united to God in the New and Eternal Covenant. Think of that the next time you walk into a church, dip your hand in the holy water, and cross yourself. With this habitual gesture, you are making the most important sign of the universe over your body—the Sign of the Cross.

From the smallest to the largest liturgical, bodily gesture, the Church is trying to awaken in you reverence for the divine. God wants holy communion with you.

During the mystery of the Mass, you enter into the sacred precincts between time and eternity, between Earth and Heaven, and between the natural and supernatural. It's all about union.

© Copyright 2019 by Monica Ashour. All rights reserved.

"The redemption of the body and, therefore, the redemption of the world, has a cosmic dimension."
Theology of the Body 86:2

The Church Points to Christ's Body

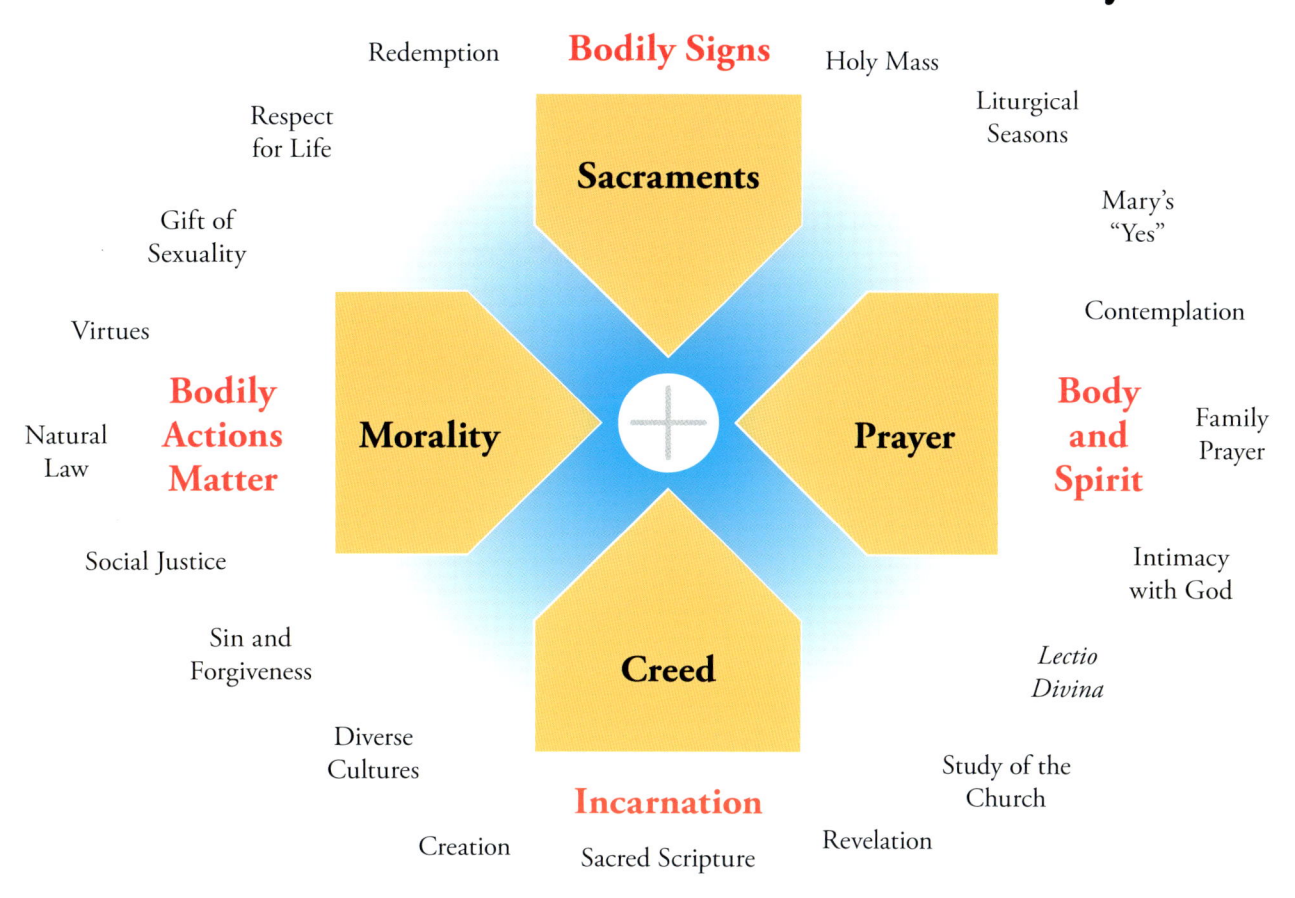

Bodily Signs

Redemption · Holy Mass · Liturgical Seasons · Respect for Life · Mary's "Yes" · Gift of Sexuality · Contemplation

Sacraments

Bodily Actions Matter

Virtues · Natural Law · Social Justice · Sin and Forgiveness

Morality

Prayer

Body and Spirit

Family Prayer · Intimacy with God · *Lectio Divina* · Study of the Church

Creed

Diverse Cultures · Creation · Sacred Scripture · Revelation

Incarnation

© Copyright 2019 by Monica Ashour. All rights reserved. "Angelo Scola, rector of the Pontifical Lateran University in Rome, goes so far as to suggest that virtually every thesis in theology—God, Christ, the Trinity, grace, the Church, the sacraments—could be seen in a new light if theologians explored in depth... John Paul II's theology of the body."—George Weigel, *Witness to Hope,* 343.

Catholicism for EveryBODY

The center of Catholicism is the Body—the Body of the Son of God. Jesus says to all, "This is My Body, given up for you." This is **the** Good News! Every single teaching the Catholic Church preserves and passes down is meant to draw you closer to the Body of Christ.

That's why the Holy Mass is the most powerful event in your life. The word *Mass* means "Go, you are sent." Having received the Body of Christ, you now have a vital mission: Live as a prophet of God's life-giving love.

The BODY matters, for it proclaims the Gospel: We are made for love by Love!

St. John Paul, a prophet proclaiming the truth of the Body.

Points to Ponder:
1. How does the solitude of Jesus on Good Friday strike you? What is significant about Holy Saturday? What impacts you about the Easter Vigil?
2. How has St. John Paul's Theology of the Body affected your view of Catholicism?

Mission: "...Glorify God in your body." 1 Cor. 6:20